Slant of Light

Jean Bodin

Slant of Light

when it comes
its echoes fade
chalked
on the sidewalk

Jean Bodin

2006-2011

©Jean Bodin 2011
Edition lulu 2011
ISBN-13: 978-1-105-56392-8
Layout: Henrico Jr.

Illustrations by the author.
Set in Linotype Avenir.

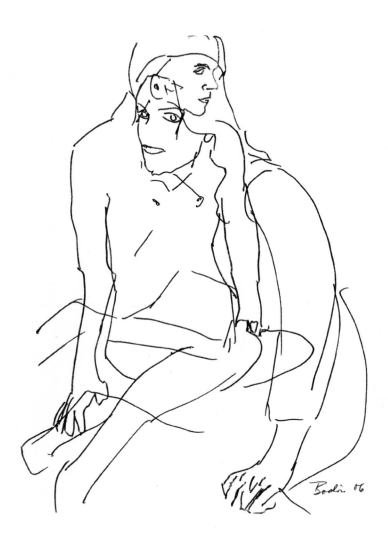

I

Hearts

between two hands
a rows barricade
crashed the silence
of the heat
but on its centre
small birds sculpted
from where we start.

Othello

I recognized
the light between my fingers
untouched by tragedy
whilst the performance moved on
but deserted before the dinner
catched fire.

Glass Menagerie

what has been
point to one end
is always present
between un-being
and the temporal
but never before
and time after.

Unseen eyebeam

invisible
doorway voices
spreading like a stain
point their fingers
in lucid stillness
to time-ridden faces
unredeemable of speculations
dignified.

Lovescape crucified

fetched in the storm
his strides bitten off
the matter with a smile
brown edged his face
like a tedious argument
in turn of tempest
done darkness until
our backs are turned
for he may not
be shaken laced in
his bower of bone.

Four times try but

as never before
he knows what the
blindfold holds
bend like a leaf

scarred hopes
outworn in witching
chords tortured
into fits

will alone
again crusted with
ice no breath
upon her hands

thousand battered words
in magic wishstone laid
can't call back the shade
the nothing that there is.

Maria@yahoo

blind silence
chases the imagination
hangs dry triumphantly
between us another
day when will it
pass untouched joy.

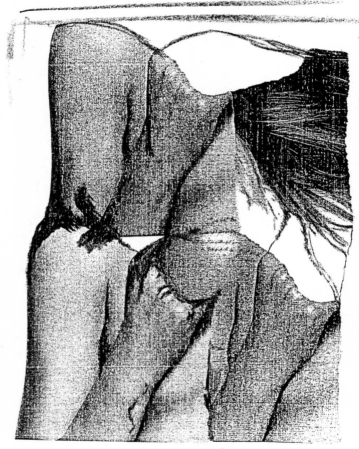

Yerma 2-09
Bodin

II

Impudent crimes

teeth
that cannot spit
whisper
neither fear nor courage
taste and touch
the moments to surrender
turn the wheels
to dry grass' singing.

Bones in whispers

walking all night in the next room
one hand on the door
like a taxi throbbing waiting

at this gliding hour
rosed wishes are set free.

Witch

thou hast nor youth nor age

her heart
among windy spaces
her words
within a word

to be beaten divided caressed
among whispers
about her harm

but me.

To notice

he ignores and creates
admixtures in meaning
demands impedes negates

provides asserts to notice
it won't heal it won't end
not even a little bit the
presence of missing terms
remains hidden but

don't throw the key away
he begs you day and night.

Iconicity or White pages of a deep dark life

she is chained
to his mind all
he wants is both
to be together
for the love she
does not find no
matters how hard
he tries coupling
images and matter
tangled into chains
infinitely or vice
versa behind them
in the city rests white in
anchors of black thirst.

Here

from here I start
and here I'm dumped
between two windows
whilst the day moves
on in the terror
of a rainy morning.

Further in

right in the middle
I am transparent
out of reach

carried in my shadow
before dissolving
like a tablet

calls loudly within
me that echoes you
blossom in space.

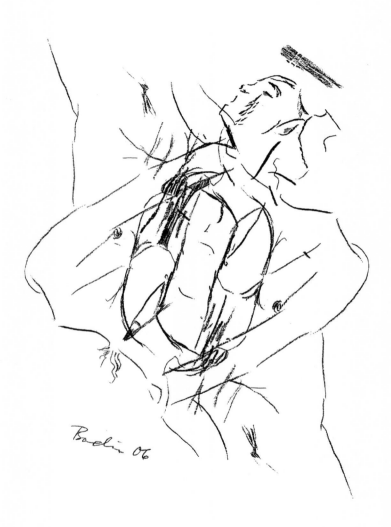

Gang bang

I feel you dawg
cause you're
so used
to being
in the hood

what are you
looking out there for?

hey dawg
straight up
you can come
to my pad

we're always
gonna be
from the hood.

Give or take

a neat freak
who mops and vacuums
his home
every day
his given you
in life
we be opened
at the judgement
and be remembered
forever.

I missed
pulling out
the gun
I like
taking risks.

Gabriel's fine line

for a while
during his transition
father G.
of a working man
Laura
he got high
scarface
to help him calm
his demons.

He & I

agony of flame
washed down
between us

in a tin
that cannot
with rusty water

singe a sleeve
ground a blade
in the whole and all.

Dust of snow

a day
I had rued

in a corner
some untidy spot
zero at the bone
life leaks away
to whirr and chime

a day
the sky suspended.

Overcoat forever

here where
the wind
is always
tortured
into fits
she felt
among the leaves
the dew
of old devotions.

Migrant eyes

the guns disturbed
the hour
a breath upon
her hand muted
the night

just as before
he went below
fleet foot
on the sill of shade
fetching

her woven scarves
the world is as
it used to be
she cried against
the elders by her side.

Yenna 2-09
Rodin

Joint project

from
flat desert to
high-rise canyon

magnet
of hot money
few wonder why

such politics are usual
having won as
one.

Don't you worry

white sox cap
the ivy league
the marine corps
the fed no one

is sure where
to turn will it
never end tangible
visual articulation.

Proofs

right now
it's no change

we can believe to
but he has to
hope
rock solid competence

we portion thereof
turns its lonely eyes
to you host of freedom

brands not
contemplated by its creators.

Merely good or evil anymore

too much
of a bad thing
to accomplish
their objectives

fervent lip with a wicked heart

delving deeply
into the true motives
like earthenware covered
with silverdoon.

Damages

if it sells
make more

to flush out
a faulty hunch
save the world
or plunder it

if they haven't already
thirtysome thing.

Roulette wheel

decline to
dispense it
broadly expended

only now
do we learn
exactly why.

Starter kit

feeding
as easy as

watering attachments
and two refills
compare and save
land home security

extended service
available.

Active persuits

end of season
save on all
treadmills
exercise cycles
elliptical trainers
& weight benches.

Northwest territory

queen-sized
raised crabgrass
packaged preventer
nonpatented coordinating
decor on sale.

Playback boy

reduced glare
unhooked dynamite

flat-screen smart
Napoleon mail-in
notorious rebate formula
escape space save

for details claim
underground duality.

Limited warranty

rust free
scratch resistant
storm patented
complete abdominal
no rain checks.

Assortment

get points

portable cash
credit persue
active check
debit adjustable
step-through design

get more

portable persuit adjustable
cash credit check debit
step-through design
transfers attempt
smooth transition.

Sale

anywhere
workout with
total range
of motion

if further
discomfort results
continue exercise
anytime.

Bullet witch

unplugged
licensed sets

high-back booster
seven years ago

employee
of the months.

Yerma's deterioration

my son
I guess
I don't have
a mother's hands
myself

killed
many nights
I go down to feed
the oxen
which I never
did before because
no women does it
I have

killed
when I pass
through the darkness
of the shed
my footsteps
sound to me
like the footsteps
of a man

I myself
have killed
my son
animals
lick them, don't they?

Lessons of the laundresses

barren
and unfertile soil
on the verge of desert

contest-grin
as yellow binds
sweet waters flowers fruits

hole prison tomb no
rain softens stones
most laundresses

come to feed
on her grief
cry where birds play.

Loyality

instructive
craving for a child
in order
to put under
light the value
of honor itself
to sacrifice
even life on the altar
reads the dramaturg

the actress
asks why should
the audience share
her choice either
a wife's
predicament to its
better end or
fragile leaf
soaked with her grief.

Lethal blow erotic

what a grey pity
to be unable
to feel the
teachings of the elderly

women

see the condom
tossed into the mud
satan
is the god of love.

Yerma's prayer

ay-y-y! looking
for my flowers
I run into a wall

the surely sullen bell
gave warning
flint and steel
where in the blood
does lightning hide
the joy so sweet

it is that wall
I'll break my head
amen.

Strategy

unknown duration
of wishes and dreams
news hope once
more hidden to
decode the unspoken.

Petticoat full of holes

lorca, brecht and riefenstahl
felt lonely had a dream I can't bear that
remain privat don't tell me

old lady if you read this line remember not
the hand that writ it for I praise you so
that in your footsteps weeds grow
coquettish as the scene goes on

noble villain regardless of family
ancestry mourning for my life
wouldn't it be better for us to part
lorca, brecht and riefenstahl?

Yerma 2 -09
Badin

VII

Neighbor's osmosis

their throat is
an open tomb
but the fight is shifted in blue-ray's favor

whose mouth is full
of cursing and bitterness
removes the speck from your brother's eye

with their tongues
they have practiced deceit
we'll decide on a case by case basis

due to
investment demand.

Mount of olives

withdrawn from his disciples
about a stone's throw
he prayed more earnestly
blood falling down to the earth

strengthened restructuring
charges sell-off skills in
deal making agreement
smoky smell of success

was there a scream
in the background
time to adjust to
impact of sales
but a gospel of judas
will excide all of them

plea for clarity.

What then?

Persecution arises for
the words sake the ones
sown among thorns
they are the ones who
hear the word no more
may be remembered
cursed is everyone who
hangs on the tree

what then shall we say?

Are we better than they?

Those who hear the words
accept it and bear fruit
but the birds
came and devoured it
by faith apart from
the deeds of the law

for there is no difference.

Significant revenue at mount zion

a cool hand
in the heat of battle
mildly surprised to come to terms
referred to
as a hedge
chained to the spirits of
just man made perfect
wary of predicting the future.

Down deep roots

stable relationship
between supply and demand
to diversify the agreement
has prompted criticism

the terms of the deal
similar to those signed
disenfranchised and under
fire expected to need prosecutors

guns go to counter.

Miracle announced

on defense over growth
the deficit is
set

the latest forecast
cast down over
the complete failure

on its promises of prosperity
no longer under a tutor
to tackle the problems.